Coping™

COPING WHEN
A PARENT HAS
A DISABILITY

Mary P. Donahue, PhD

Rosen
YA™

New York

Thanks to Molly and her family, as they are not only the inspiration for this book, but also provide hope as role models in their community.

Published in 2019 by The Rosen Publishing Group, Inc.
29 East 21st Street, New York, NY 10010

Expert Reviewer: H. Ace Ratcliff, disability rights activist

Library of Congress Cataloging-in-Publication Data

Names: Donahue, Mary P., author.
Title: Coping when a parent has a disability / Mary P. Donahue, PhD
Description: New York : Rosen Publishing, 2019 | Series: Coping | Audience: Grades 7–12. | Includes bibliographical references and index.
Identifiers: LCCN 2017051967| ISBN 9781508178965 (library bound) | ISBN 9781508178958 (pbk.)
Subjects: LCSH: Children of parents with disabilities—Juvenile literature.
Classification: LCC HQ759.912 .D66 2018 | DDC 306.874087—dc23
LC record available at https://lccn.loc.gov/2017051967

Manufactured in the United States of America

CONTENTS

INTRODUCTION

Becoming a teenager is hard! In addition to the work of everyday living, adolescence is a time for you to figure out who you are and where you fit in. And life can be complicated all on its own. Forget that everyone else is trying to tackle the same stuff. Overwhelming might be an understatement!

Everyone has challenges: social skills, school, athletics, love, acne, and other things. What if yours include some home life issues, like having a parent with a disability? How could that affect your teen years? What do you need to know? And what can you do about it?

First, meet Molly. She is fifteen years old, and her dad has schizophrenia, which is a serious mental illness. He stays in the house a lot; he can't work, and he can't be around a lot of people. He doesn't always understand what's going on around him. Things can go pretty wrong for him, so Molly's mom stays home to care for him and the family. Her mom doesn't sleep that much, especially when her dad's symptoms are intense. Mom's also responsible for all the kids' appointments, school support, groceries, meals, and so on. The family is living in poverty. Food and medications take priority over things like cell phones, new clothes, and bikes. Life can be pretty rough. Sometimes, Molly doesn't know what to expect for the day, or even the next

It's not always easy to cope with having a disabled parent, but it's important to get out and enjoy adventures together, like going to the ocean.

hour. Sometimes, she misses school or isn't able to do homework because her dad's illness is the top concern. Some kids say awful things about her family. Some are afraid to be friends with her.

Still, Molly's older brother is a talented athlete and class president. Molly herself can play six different instruments and has been invited to play with orchestras. Her younger sibling is an artist with mad skills already, and the youngest of all is "the best storyteller!" Molly says her father is very funny and gives great hugs. Her mom "is the strongest, most loving woman I know." Molly fights with her siblings, but when necessary, they have each other's back. What makes Molly and her family so tight? In spite of a challenging and sometimes unpredictable home life, how do all the members of her family keep achieving their goals?

Having a parent whose body, thinking patterns, or abilities are outside of commonly experienced routines can have an effect on how people treat your parent and you. As you might already know, growing kids often mimic adult behaviors around them, sometimes without thinking. This can lead to harsh judgments. Also, sometimes people use any little difference in others to criticize, belittle, or dismiss them. Some people pick on these differences because it gives them power. Others don't know they're doing it. Although you wish that people could see their hurtful behavior and stop it, that's not the reality. So, because nobody can control the thoughts of another, it's better to focus on yourself, what's happening now, and how you can feel empowered to accept your experiences and ride with them. You'll then have more choices and ultimately more control over your life. It's hard work, and it can be really worth it.

CHAPTER ONE

Definitions and Dangers

What is a disability? It's a weird word because it implies that a person's difference is a negative or disadvantage in his or her life. Dictionaries define it as "a lack of adequate power or strength." The Social Security Administration says that people are disabled if they are "not able to engage in any substantial gainful activity." The Americans with Disability Act (1990) looks at disability as "a physical or mental impairment that significantly limits one or more major life activities." Overall, though, types of disabilities are considered in areas such as:

- Hearing
- Vision
- Movement
- Cognition (thinking)
- Mood (feeling)
- Self-care

and other things typically seen as necessary for independent living. It can get frustrating, though, because different agencies have different criteria for different people. So some people may be termed disabled at one place but not in another; they may be entitled to considerations in some places but not in others. Some disabilities aren't visible, so their needs can be harder to explain. And many people are afraid even to talk directly to a disabled person.

Just Ask

Sometimes, for people who are not disabled, how to respectfully describe someone who is disabled can be confusing. There are varying preferences, and no one wants to insult another person. Recent research indicates that there are two main ways to refer to a disabled person. One is called person-first language. That's when the speaker focuses on the person ahead of the disability. So, for instance, instead of "disabled person," you might say "person with a disability," or "girl who is blind."

The second way is called identity-first language, which considers the other person's identity as a disabled person—similar to how others might see themselves as a tall person, a Christian person, or

This mom and daughter are using sign language to communicate. If you are unfamiliar with it, don't be afraid to ask about it.

a smart person. Of course, in social situations, the disabled person's name generally does the trick! How can you know which way is preferred? Don't hesitate to ask. It's the respectful thing to do.

Perhaps in part because of that kind of confusion, mainstream society doesn't always stop to think. It continues to do things the way it usually has. For example, public buildings don't always have ramp access to the front door; not all businesses have specialized telephone equipment for the hearing impaired; academic accommodations aren't always available; insurance sometimes doesn't cover needed materials and services. Even though the law requires things for people with disabilities, those things sometimes aren't there.

Consider this, though: nearly one in five adults (20 percent) aged twenty-five to forty-four are classified in the 2010 US Census as having a disability. As well, there are currently between 4.1 and 9 million parents who have a disability. That means there are more than 4.1 million kids who are living with a parent with disabilities. And these numbers are rising due to events like interpersonal violence and war. That's a lot of adults who don't fit the so-called typical mold. So, an intriguing question is: are disabled people disadvantaged because of their differing physical or mental functioning or because society isn't as accommodating as it needs to be? Couldn't disability be more a question of convenience for the status quo?

Stigma

In thinking about the status quo, consider the stigma of disability. When people's functioning or interests are outside of the mainstream, others often devalue them. For those who are disabled, the disability is likely just a part of who they are. But others might see

Crutches serve as walking aids, a means to get around and enjoy a little sun. Sadly, many see crutches and the disabilities that might necessitate their use as negative characteristics.

them as inferior and the disability as negative. This is considered a stigma of disability. People who don't know better are afraid or uninformed. They may avoid a stigmatized person, even looking right past them. The person with a disability is often belittled or blamed for something he or she didn't ask for. And then, of course, there are the people who really want to help, but the resources aren't available. Thus, it is the disabled person who is most affected. Because of stigma, people with disabilities can lose out on jobs, social activities, and a sense of personal accomplishment. By association, some people may be uncomfortable talking to you, too, if your parent has a disability. Whether hoping not to insult you, trying to overdo it in helping you, fearing they may catch what your parent has (really!), or simply being ill informed, their reaction to you can be frustrating!

Thinking Errors

Next, consider thinking errors, because some people you run into seem to have them. You probably do, too, by the way. According to psychologist Aaron Beck, thinking errors are unhelpful ways of thinking that increase stress, anxiety, and depression. There are many, but the following are three that might be particularly important for you to understand.

All or Nothing

This kind of thinking happens when someone sees traits or situations as all good or all bad. Some kids think, for example, that if they have pimples, they're ugly, they're stupid, and no one will ever love them! Others might think that because a kid doesn't move like others do, he isn't worth having on a team. In

Bullies are intimidating, and without training, your mind could go anywhere. Remember that there is help and support out there, and if at first you don't succeed, try again!

short, because one thing isn't typical, there is no value anywhere else. Be careful if you're thinking this. For example, Molly needed help trying to get a bully off her back. The first few times she told her mother, it was really chaotic in the house, so her mom didn't get it. Molly could have just given up because her voice sometimes gets lost when stuff goes wrong at home. She could have thought something like, "No one will ever care. I'm alone in the world." This is the if-something-doesn't-work-once-it-will-never-work attitude. Of course, if that were true, we wouldn't have airplanes, the internet, or even WD-40!

Mind Reading

The mind-reading thinking error happens when people assume they know what another person is thinking. It's a problem because people start to think things like "those kids must pity me" and then change their actions (like passing on a club they really want to join) just to avoid what they assume others are thinking. This robs people of growing experiences that are not only potentially helpful but possibly fun.

Unreal Ideal

The unreal ideal is common among teens. It involves making unfair comparisons between ourselves and others. Some teens feel they have to be the strongest or most buff or have the best clothes or best grades.

Even when they're rocking something, they feel it isn't enough! Often, the best, or even what you think is adequate, just isn't possible. It's unreal. With this kind of thinking, embarrassment and shame can set in before you know it. Then the other two thinking errors set in, and you might think, "If I'm not measuring up, nothing ever works right and everyone will always be looking at me as a loser!" These thinking errors tend to kill motivation and steal joy from life.

Wrapping and Relating ...

So, when considering statistics, stigma, and thinking errors, it appears that having a disabled parent may be a matter of perception: differences versus status quo. If so, that's good news! Because thinking like that means there's parity in what you and your family can expect: a right to equality. Knowing this can shift the frame of mind with which you approach life at this point. Your parent and you might be made to feel *less than* for having different needs. Maybe you don't make your needs known. Parity, though, shows you that you do have empowering options. Consider this: Molly's father can't go to parent-teacher meetings because they're currently conducted during chaotically busy Parents Night, where he would become overwhelmed, get confused, and leave the school. Molly and her mom asked her teachers for private appointment

This student and her dad have learned how to keep asking for what she needs, which can be a pretty helpful skill!

times to review Molly's work, outside of Parents Night. Some teachers were accepting. Others got touchy about it, sighing and making a face. At first, Molly got the message that her needs were burdensome. Who wouldn't want to avoid that? So, for several years, her dad couldn't go. However, once Molly and her parents learned how to ask for their needs to be met and believed they should be met, guess what happened? They made goals, developed a team, researched her rights, and presented their need. Now her dad goes to her reworked Student Review sessions whenever he can.

Molly and her family learned a lot from this experience. They learned about the basic rights of children, what that means, and how to explain it. They learned about cultural competency for service providers. Cultural competency is the ability to honor and respect the differences of people and their families who require nonmainstream services. Again, because providers are often misinformed, overworked, or undersupported, they can forget to take a moment and think about the actual person who's before them; they respond the way they usually do. You have the right to ask—respectfully—for a provider to focus on you, specifically, and for your needs to be met.

The Choice for a Voice

Yes, you have rights. While you hear a lot about basic human and civil rights for adults, you might not know that there's a whole movement in the world working on children's rights. Here's a quick list of some rights for US teens:

- To have access to both parents (unless the court has intervened)

Take the time to get to know your school administrator. If you get confused or need help with a big issue, you'll know whom to seek out.

- To be safe
- To explore and express their identity
- To have basic needs met, such as physical protection, food, education, health care access, play, and recreation

Essentially, regardless of your background, you have the same right to develop your potential as every other US kid. But things that can result from having a parent with a disability, including lack of access to accommodations, inconsistent school attendance, and the need to slow down, among other things, means that lots of kids get lost—can be invisible—in a system where required but nonmainstream needs are sometimes overlooked. So, although you have a right to have a voice in matters concerning you, this is news to many children, parents, agencies, and administrators. When there's no voice, there are considerably fewer choices in life. Remember, unless people are made aware of and/or taught new ways, they continue to do things the way they've always been done. To help you assert yourself, you need to consider the terms "empathy" and "respect," while contemplating three categories of disability and some considerations in each one.

Myths & FACTS

Myth: Disabled people are fakers.

Fact: The vast majority of people who claim a disability are forthright. Negative opinions can be found anywhere. Although there certainly are some people who know how to cheat the system, it is not easy to fake a disability for benefits. More than 60 percent of people who apply for disability are denied. Wouldn't it be great if you could contribute to the discussion for thoughtful, informed truth?

Myth: Children of disabled parents are always kids in need.

Fact: Many people see disability as burdensome and imagine all that a kid must be lacking. In truth, many kids with disabled parents develop a unique way of seeing the world that can include helpful empathy, effective problem solving, creativity, self-advocacy, and valuable career direction.

Myth: Disabled people cannot be active community members.

Fact: Think about Harriet Tubman, Franklin Roosevelt, Michelangelo, Albert Einstein, Stevie Wonder, Cher, Jazzie Collins, Stephen Hawking, Alice Walker, Tony Coelho, and so on. All these highly achieving, world-changing people had at least one form of disability. Many people just need a chance to have their needs met; then they might soar!

CHAPTER TWO

Same and Different, All at Once

To get what you need, you'll sometimes have to find a way to engage people who would rather keep you at a distance. Maybe more confusing for you, though, is someone with a disability, such as your parent, who also seems to push you away. You might feel hurt. It's asking a lot for you not to take it personally. However, by using your imagination to look for reasons other than the obvious one, maybe you can understand both sides (yours and your parent's) better.

That being said, it should help you to try and see things from your parent's perspective so you can better understand how her disability might affect her and why she's responding to you as she is. You're busy being a kid and doing kid stuff. In a

Wear Different Shoes

An important part of coping is developing empathy. That's when you learn to put yourself "in the shoes" of someone else. It's a helpful skill because then you can imagine what the thoughts, feelings, and experiences of another might be like from that person's perspective. It takes you out of your own head and opens up possibilities. When you can see more sides to a story, you can consider other reasons why someone might react to you the way they do. This helps you make better decisions about how to respond, in ways for which you'll feel proud. Empathy skills increase communication tools and emotional stability. Empathy saves energy, too. It's key to good health.

perfect world, at this age you should be able to explore yourself more. You're developing your individuality. Having to put yourself on hold to attend to someone else doesn't seem fair. It's tempting to ignore family needs or forget the struggles of your parent. Just because you don't want to think about something, though, doesn't mean it doesn't exist, right? Take a look at some general categories of disabilities and what those might mean to you or your parent.

Physical Disabilities

When people think of physical disabilities, they usually think of obvious physical signs like missing or unusually held limbs, wheelchairs, and white canes. These are often accepted disabilities because they pass a "vision test," as in the disabilities can be seen. However, there are also less visually noticeable physical disabilities, such as heart disease, skeletal problems, fibromyalgia, multiple sclerosis, and many other physically exhausting diseases. Regardless of the genesis, though, physically operating in a mainstream environment is challenging. For example, think about getting somewhere. What special considerations do you think a physically disabled person has to deal with? Besides the extra time needed in the morning routine, think about things like curb heights. Many mobility devices are stopped by curbs. Some people have poor depth perception. Crosswalks, too, can be difficult. Many don't have lights or bells to tell people when to cross; drivers don't always see pedestrians crossing. Then there are access points that may be blocked by construction or big puddles. Weather is tricky, too. Buses don't always stop where they're supposed to, and parking can be problematic, because nondisabled people sometimes park in spots reserved for the disabled. All of this means more complicated travel to a safe crossing area. Jaywalking can be deadly!

A cane can help someone to feel around for obstacles and orienting signals in front of him. It also helps seeing people to know to take care.

Access problems are also difficult for more basic daily needs such as using the restroom. Many old office buildings have made accommodations inside the restroom within the original building structure, but door width can be a problem. And sometimes there's a two-door entry for privacy, with a small space between the doors. Try negotiating that on a good day, let alone when there are hurried people, two-way traffic, and no automatic door openers.

Once inside the restroom, a disabled person might find a stall with a larger moving-around space, balance bars, and so on. This would accommodate walking aids and instability—if that big stall isn't occupied by someone who is in a hurry or maybe isn't sensitive to the reason for a larger stall. After using the toilet, the person would have to figure out how to wash his hands. The sink might not be close enough or might require two hands to push on the spigot. There may be water all over the counter from previous users, so if the person leans in, he gets wet. Or he may have to put his hands on the watery counter to

This bathroom sign seems simple enough. But for a disabled person, using public restrooms can be fraught with challenges.

see or to feel for what he wants to do. And where are the hand dryers or towel dispensers—assuming there is more than one? It's tough to navigate a wheelchair with wet hands, making the move from sink to hand-drying area extremely difficult. Plus, public restrooms are all different. All of this takes time and brainpower to negotiate. And that's just to use the restroom! Forget office things like navigating a cubicle, making copies, carrying files, or sitting at a table. Being employed, going to appointments, going out socially—it all takes so much time and consideration that nondisabled people just don't have to think about.

Mental Health and Other Brain Disabilities

People experiencing mental health and brain disabilities often encounter similar challenges with time and mobility. One particularly difficult and hidden aspect of mental health and brain disabilities is called psychophobia. This is when someone has an illogical fear about things affecting the mind, often stemming from observing curious actions. It's a form of prejudice. The actions of a psychophobic can negatively affect you, for example, in terms of denying services, being rude, or avoiding interacting with you. In addition, because so little is known about the brain in general, symptoms of many mental health and brain disabilities vary among individuals. People are afraid of or annoyed by what they don't understand. So the mainstream doesn't know what to expect. That makes it harder to understand. It makes it harder for your parent—and maybe you—to accept, too.

But the mental health and brain disabilities population is pretty big. According to the National Alliance on Mental Illness, about 10 percent of people aged eighteen to forty-nine (common parenting age) have a serious mental health issue; one in six people have a developmental disability; and a serious brain injury happens about every twenty-three seconds. That's a lot of people with potential mental and physical disabilities.

Both physical and mental disabilities must be considered. Following is a list of some brain-based issues that are often unseen:

- Traumatic brain injuries resulting from damage to the brain caused by an external force
- Learning disabilities, such as language or auditory processing, nonverbal language disorders, or attention-deficit disorders
- Intellectual disabilities, such as fetal alcohol syndrome, autism, or developmental delays
- Mental illnesses, such as schizophrenia, bipolar disorder, major depression, or post-traumatic stress disorders

As with physical disabilities, when the brain is affected by mental health and brain disabilities, life-complicating situations arise. Things like memory loss and confusion, headache, attention and focus skills, balance, emotional regulation, vision problems, and planning and decision making can be affected. For people with mental health and brain disabilities, simple things like encountering road construction can get tricky real fast.

Extra Complications

Every person only has a certain amount of mental energy at any given time. No matter how much you have to do or what is going on in your life, you only have so much energy to use in dealing with it. You can't create more energy; you have to take it from somewhere else in your life. Sometimes, you feel totally overwhelmed with more to do and think about than you have energy for. So maybe you "lose it" and yell or snap at people or withdraw to somewhere no one can bother you. Or maybe you do worse. When this happens, try to put off some activities and give yourself time to regroup. Hopefully, you get to choose what to give up. A disabled person, though, often doesn't get to choose how to navigate the world. Each added complication requires more energy. That energy has to be taken from somewhere else; consideration is

When you are frustrated, try to ask for help, and try to give yourself some time and space to regroup, rather than lashing out at others—or yourself.

necessary. Empathy can really help. Two more components can require a disabled person to spend even more energy than you can imagine: hidden disabilities and sudden disabilities.

Hidden Disabilities

Many forms of disability cannot be seen, such as heart problems or autoimmune diseases. Some individuals might have thought disorders or impulse-control problems. People with invisible disabilities have disabilities others cannot immediately see. The complication this adds, however, is that other people tend to judge things immediately, without thinking. Thus, a heart patient who parks in a disabled spot can be a target for snide comments or rude notes left on the windshield. If an invisibly disabled person asked someone on the bus for a seat, nastiness may happen. What's more, the mainstream sometimes dismisses what it doesn't see. It doubts that it's real or thinks the person is angling for an advantage

It can be difficult to cope when your parent looks fine on the outside but struggles with an invisible disability, such as an autoimmune disease like multiple sclerosis or a heart problem.

through special treatment. These actions fuel mistrust. Thus, hidden disabilities can put your parent in a lose-lose situation; either she endures added hardship or she reveals very private, personal health information. It can be hard for you, too, because you're not always sure what to tell people. You might want to smooth your parent's way, but you don't want the added misunderstandings that can come with doing so. You might feel protective but don't want to risk exposure. And always explaining things is a big energy drain.

Sudden Disability

The second special consideration in disability is the difficulty presented when a parent has a sudden onset of a disability. Maybe a dad had a brain injury, or a mom's leg was amputated. Maybe an existing illness like multiple sclerosis or major depression has gotten worse. Whatever it is, your parent may not be able to think or move like he's used to doing. While your family once had a routine and enjoyed lots of regular life experiences, everything changed in an instant. Family members have to learn new ways of doing things. This uses energy they have to take from other places. And there are things that you may not be able to do anymore, either, like having algebra help, a running partner, or someone to help keep your schedule. You might try to explain something rough that happened at school, but your parent is asking too many questions and messing

Some disabilities happen suddenly, such as when someone has to have his legs amputated. His new legs probably took some getting used to before he could trust them.

up details. You may have to do more chores or miss more school or functions to help in other ways. It's frustrating for both you and your parent.

There is a certain amount of grief that you have to deal with. Energy you're supposed to use for growing and figuring out teen life has to be rerouted. You might have feelings of guilt or shame; you're frustrated but don't want to dis your parent. You love her. Or you don't want to look like a jerk. Some kids swallow the frustration. Some parents do, too. This can lead to even more complicating issues, like silent anger or resentment, substance use, and trouble at school or with friends. Your whole world might have turned upside down. Everything seems more confusing. You're growing physically and hopefully maturing mentally. You might be worried about how to handle the different pressures of a typical teenage life combined with an atypical challenge of a nonmainstream family life. How do you do that? What do you need to know? Fortunately, there are certain things to watch out for and skills you'll want to develop.

Many Paths, but to Where?

CHAPTER THREE

Up until this point in your natural, everyday development, you've been exploring your world, learning to please, acquiring skills, and absorbing the rules of life. Going from middle school to high school is where you put it all together. You strengthen your sense of self, personal values, and communication styles. Caretakers don't have to be as observant of your needs anymore, and you learn to connect things for yourself. Also, while life lessons up to this point might have come from family life, your job now is to venture out and find where you fit into the world. This often produces great frustration. Remember, you have a finite amount of personal energy, so learning to prioritize life's demands is essential—and sometimes exhausting. It's helpful to know what you're working with both typically and in your particular circumstances.

Privacy or Secrecy?

These terms might seem similar, but they're actually opposites. Privacy is when you have details—or whole stories—that belong to you. You get to tell them when, if, and why you choose, but everyone doesn't have to know. Secrecy is about avoiding pain. It's driven by fear and often by shame. It takes a lot of energy to keep a secret, and the fear of being found out is exhausting. It pushes people away. Secrecy takes away choice; privacy allows a sense of self. Learning to accept yourself, your parent, and your situation, and sharing only when you feel it's safe and appropriate, provides relief and more freedom. Who can't use that?

First, know that it's natural for you to want to test limits and seek more control over your life. You're more influenced now by media and peer groups than when you were little. Biological changes may make you moody and sometimes lead to body aches from growing organs and bones. You might find yourself switching from having high expectations of yourself to feelings of failure. Confidence is elusive. Especially in early adolescence, teens tend to make risky choices

Friends give and get healthy support from each other. It's important, especially when faced with tough challenges, to reach out for help and encouragement.

without thinking of consequences. You'll probably learn to develop deeper relationships with friends or romantic partners. There's less hugging with your family and more with your friends. You'll likely begin to solidify your sexual identity and preferences. As well, you're probably making new friends while others fall away. These are all typical developmental tasks. You may not know to where, but you're on your way!

In addition to the natural things happening in your life, you individually have a unique mix of extra ingredients, as most teens do. For example, some kids have a parent in the military, have a single parent or blended household, are food insecure, change schools a lot, or are homeschooled. As you can imagine, each of these situations creates its own group of unique challenges, all competing for energy. Successful adjustment begins with being able to identify factors, both natural and individualized, that affect your developing life. Once you do that, you have a better idea of where you're going and what to look out for. Below are a few things you should know about: watching out for codependency, creating healthy boundaries, and negotiation.

Codependency in Youth

Depending on what kind of disability a parent has and how he or she experiences it, a family learns to

It's easy to feel overwhelmed and that there just isn't enough time in the day to get everything done! These are times to review the "have-to" list.

react in the moment as necessary. Sometimes, these reactive behaviors can turn into an unhealthy type of functioning called codependency. In other words, you become so focused on your parent's problems that you put aside your own. You might try to control who comes over, what notes your parent sees, or how much medication he takes. Maybe you don't tell him

41

things he should know but you think will upset him. You worry a lot when you're not with your parent, wondering if he's OK. You're so focused on him that your schoolwork suffers, you have no time for friends or events, and you lose sleep. Even if you could tell someone, you wouldn't know how. There might also be family rules that prevent you from openly expressing emotions. You might be feeling overburdened by life (which is typical in adolescence), and you want to scream or run away for a little while—but you can't. You feel strong pressure to conform, and you swallow your own needs. You do what you think you're *supposed* to do—avoid problems and take care of who needs to be taken care of.

After a while, you forget which needs belong to whom. You might become overprotective of your family members and not protective enough of yourself. You learn to anticipate what you think your parent needs and feel expected to provide it. You forget about you. Eventually, you develop a false self—a person who does and says what she's supposed to and denies what she really feels. You still have needs and feelings of your own, but you keep pushing them away. You check up on things that shouldn't be your responsibility. You work harder for someone else's comfort than you do for your own. You begin feeling isolated, confused, or like you're invisible. There's anger and bitterness, and you have no effective way to communicate it. So you keep doing what you're expected to do—or at least you think so. You're not sure anymore.

Codependency is a complicated issue. It's seldom discussed, so few teens know about it. When something isn't recognized, it is more likely to happen because you're not looking out for it. Moreover, if your parent has a disability, you sometimes have to do adult things with a kid brain. You might feel expected to be an adult before you're ready. You might have to make doctor's appointments, drive to them, listen and remember medical information, and write the checks to pay for them. You might have to decline regular teen events like sports or prom—which can be important to social development—because you think it's too expensive or you'll be needed at home. On a bad day, you may find yourself consoling your parent or sibling instead of yourself. You may feel responsible for getting your siblings on the bus and helping with homework, cooking, or medications; school decisions might fall to you regularly. Many of these things can't be changed. You have to do them. You can choose different ways to deal with these things, however, and there's probably a chance for negotiation of boundaries—with your parent, social circle, and yourself. This is important. Healthy relationships depend on healthy boundaries.

Personal Boundaries

You may hear the word "boundary" a lot, but what does it really mean? Think of it like a fence. It has two purposes: to keep things in and to keep things out. On a farm, for instance, a fence can keep cows in the pasture and deer out of the garden. In other words, boundaries are for protecting what's valuable. Socially, boundaries are necessary because you are valuable.

Upon reviewing codependency, you can see that it comes from lack of good boundaries. In a codependent relationship, you don't know where you start and where the other person ends. You lose yourself. Boundaries help you separate your own thoughts and feelings from those of others. They give you a sense of containment in that you know your own personal value system—what you're willing to do for yourself and others as well as how you agree to be treated by them. In this way, you can contribute to relationships that are mutually respectful.

Boundaries give a sense of security and comfort. For example, if you know how far you're willing to go to help people, then you also know when to stop helping. You'll know where you stand. You'll know when you're trying too hard, when you're spending more energy on someone else's needs than on your own, and when others are treating you in hurtful ways. Boundaries are a way of valuing yourself. And, if you don't value yourself, how can you expect others to?

Knowing what you're responsible for in your life and allowing others to be responsible for themselves is also a really healthy way of respecting others. Allow them the chance to see what they're capable of, which can add to their own sense of self-worth. That doesn't mean you can never help out; it means you just have to know when the cost is greater than the benefit. It's hard to honor a boundary when someone else is pressuring you, but after a few times of holding firm, people tend to respect it—or at least, they stop asking. Those who love you will stay, and those who were using you will go. That can't be bad.

Finally, some people have poor boundaries because they feel it's selfish to take care of themselves first. Let's say that you've been going straight out for a week with no downtime. It's Sunday, and all you want to do is hang out with your cat and play some video games. But your friend calls. He's lonely and just wants to come over for a few hours. Those are the only few hours you have for yourself. But he sounds really depressed and you technically do have the time. What can you do? With poor boundaries, you invite him over. He comes and overstays, but he feels better when he leaves. You're glad to have helped, but there's a lot on your mind, and you'll start another busy week

Protect your personal resources. When you give away your time, you can't get it back, leaving you with even less energy than you thought you would have.

still being exhausted. This might lead to less ability to focus, being short tempered, and not doing your best work. Then you'll spend more energy fixing things you messed up. You gave up caring for yourself in favor of helping someone else, but it cost too much. And by Thursday, your friend is sad or bored and calls again. And again.

So, regarding selfishness, imagine the fence again. If the farmer had no fence, the deer would come and happily eat the vegetables. The farmer will have fed some hungry deer. Or she could put up a fence, protect her crop, harvest it, and keep what she needs. Then she can give or trade the rest away—by her own choice and according to what is best for her own goals. Was the fence selfish or a useful boundary? Time and energy are valuable resources and need to be protected.

Responsibility for Self

People often do things because other people want them to. They let others make decisions for them. The problem with that, though, is the "consequence rule." This rule says that regardless of intent, the person who acts is the one who will be responsible for the outcome. So, if your friends want you to lie to your parents and attend a party, they're not the ones who will pay for that action if you get caught. You are. That's why it's always best to do and be what you think is best for you. Be yourself, rather than who others want you to be. The results belong to you either way.

Negotiation

Taking into account what you now know about codependency and boundaries, you might be wondering how to go about developing boundaries to avoid codependency. That can happen through negotiation. But beware: some people think the purpose of personal negotiation is to win. It isn't. It's about finding mutual ground for managing conflicting needs. Say there are two things that really need to

The goal of negotiating is not just to win. An important part of the negotiation process is to take the time to listen to one another's concerns.

get done but time schedules conflict; you might use negotiation skills to meet both needs.

Take a look at Molly again. She really wanted to join an after-school group that she felt would benefit her musical skills. Unfortunately, her mother needed her at home after school to meet her siblings at the bus stop, as she had been doing for the past two years. Initially, Molly was annoyed that she had to decline the group's invitation. But as she thought about it, she realized there might be room for negotiation. Maybe both needs could be addressed. So, she gathered all the facts about her and her older brother's schedule. She also identified a neighborhood friend who went to the same school as her siblings. She came up with possible solutions for the two days a week she'd be at the group. Then she sat with her parents and presented her problem and her plan.

First, Molly noted what she does in the house to help out. (She made sure she didn't sound like she was complaining, just telling the facts.) She was also clear about what she wanted, which was two afternoons per week to attend group meetings and some performance days. She gave possible solutions, like her brother helping, talking to the neighbor kid's parent who is usually at the bus stop, even seeing if the bus could stop a little closer to their house. Her parents were hesitant at first because they'd gotten used to a schedule that worked, and change was hard for Molly's dad. Talking through the negotiation process, however, they realized that everyone had been growing and changing and that Molly needed more freedom. They engaged her brother for one day a week and began the process of teaching the younger kids skills for walking home on their own or with the neighbor. Molly's dad was reluctant, but he agreed to give her plan a try. And Molly appreciated both herself for having rethought things and her family members for listening and working together. She felt more in control of herself because she didn't stuff down her needs, and she worked with her family to get both goals met.

As you move through high school and get ready for your adult life, learning to avoid becoming codependent by developing boundaries and negotiation skills is a great way to practice self-care. These skills allow you to have more choices in your life because you have more control over it. Combine that with empathy, and you're able to find lots of possible solutions. When you place value on how you live your life, within reason, you will feel less stressed, less overwhelmed, and more emotionally balanced.

CHAPTER FOUR

Hard Work, Major Payoff

At a time when teens are supposed to be enjoying the last years before the demands of adulthood kick in, having a parent with a disability means you have to make compromises. Sometimes, negotiations fail. Maybe your parent has surgery, her symptoms get worse, or bullies set their sights on you. Things get interrupted. Sometimes, you might feel so overwhelmed that you can't see out of it. Parental disability often causes hard life situations. Without enough support, you can end up feeling isolated, confused, depressed, or angered by your parent's disability and its effect on your life. Then guilt and shame kick in.

But it's really OK to have a bad day, when you want to just stick your head under your pillow. You're not a superhero—no one is. Still, stress isn't always a bad thing. Lots of challenged kids develop healthy skills and build satisfying lives. Fortunately, research

Sometimes you just need to take time off. An important part of self-support is to know when to stand down, especially after a bad day.

has revealed some common factors involved in helping children develop a trait called resilience. In basic terms, resilience is a person's ability to bounce back from highly stressful experiences. Growing resilience is an ongoing process, with each challenge helping build increased strength and better recovery. Following are some helpful characteristics that you can begin working on.

53

Adaptive Responses

Because resilience can continue to grow as you do, it's important to think about adaptive responses to tough stuff. Something that is adaptive works for you and helps you successfully manage your environment. Many disabled people are great at adaptive responses. Everyone has some level of adaptation to the environment, and as the environment changes, the adaptations do, too. Adaptive skills are needed by people to function every day in settings like school, home, work, the athletic field, math club, or a volunteer job. They're skills that allow you to take care of yourself and to interact with others in order to reach goals.

A key is to find out what helps you best in your time of need and develop that more. For example, some students wait until the last minute before getting to work on a paper. They might need high pressure to write good work. Others might work better in groups or prefer making creative presentations rather than writing papers. Different people have different challenges and meet them (or don't) according to their current ability. If they don't have the adaptive skills necessary for successful behavior, they can either develop them or change what they want. It all begins with curiosity, though.

For example, after Molly had a bad day dealing with her father, she began to wonder. She knew other kids with really hard stressors, like one with a drug-addicted parent, another whose parent was "in jail again," and even a kid who was an orphan. She wondered what it was about the kids she saw who seemed to handle their hard situation pretty well. She also saw teens who appeared to feel ashamed of their circumstances, while others came to school hoping and praying that they wouldn't be embarrassed that day. Molly would never have guessed that some kids she knew experienced major problems if she didn't know about the problems firsthand. What was it about these teens that caused them to persevere?

Factors in Resilience

Research by Harvard University and other well-respected institutions has been able to identify several factors that contribute to adaptive responses regarding unusually high stress:

- Modifying biological factors
- Having at least one trustworthy, stable, consistent adult relationship (for teamwork)
- Growing emotional maturity
- Developing a sense of self-confidence through situations that produce feelings of accomplishment, value, and empowerment
- Believing in yourself and your skills, and having realistic dreams for your future

Don't underestimate the power of self-confidence, which can help you feel capable, respected, and empowered, even in difficult situations.

If this list seems confusing or impossible, the good news is that you are not all on your own. Developing resiliency is important, and it is best done with a team of interested people who can offer you (and each other) safety, support, opportunity, and direction. It's hard work, and the payoff will be with you through the rest of your life.

The Myth of Fair

"That's not fair!" is something you might say when things don't go the way you think they should. Here's a fact to change your perspective: fairness is what's called a relative term. It means something different to everyone. What's fair for you may not be fair to another. Fair doesn't mean equal. If you've waited in line a long time, it's fair that you get served. It's not fair to the salesperson who has to work later because of the long line. But it's the same situation. So, instead of getting angry when something isn't fair, try to consider other viewpoints. Using your empathy tool and learning to manage disappointment is vital to making forward movement in life. Learn from the outcome and keep an open mind. You'll get there!

No Time like the Present

Each of the resilience-building factors is important, and if you don't have some, don't worry. It's never too late.

Biological Factors

Some people think they're born with what they're born with and they don't have much control over brain structure. Not true, and you learned it here first! You can indeed influence biological factors in a number of cool ways. For example, the body has what is commonly referred to as a fight-or-flight mechanism; it can sense danger and respond by fighting or running (or sometimes freezing.) That level of interpreting danger can be altered in a variety of ways. Because the brain (which is responsible for sensing your situation) has natural chemicals that activate under certain conditions, you are able to change some of that chemical activation through things like healthy relationships, regular exercise, certain kinds of physical and mental health therapy, and mindfulness or meditation.

One (or More) Healthy, Consistent Adult on Your Team

It's important for you to find an adult who can listen objectively. This may or may not be your parent. Talking is really important because it will help you feel.

They say "laughter is the best medicine" for a reason, so remember to take time for some goofy fun. It's important to allow yourself some time for lighthearted connection.

It's well known that people who cut off their feelings have poorer life outcomes; feelings contribute to wisdom. They also give flavor and color to life. Think about it: laughter doesn't happen without feelings. Joy, gladness, excitement, love, and peace are all feelings.

And without sadness, anger, disappointment, and fear, you really can't hope to know when the good feelings come along. Humans need all sorts of feelings. Having a supportive adult or two on your team helps you consider things and come up with safe, useful solutions to challenges of the day.

Emotional Maturity

Emotional maturity can be developed through emotion regulation. As great as feelings are, it's important to know how to direct them. Surely, you know people who respond to problems with extreme and public drama. They get upset about things as if it's the worst thing ever! Their responses are so quick and intense that they miss lots of information that could completely change the meaning of a situation. Having skills that help you take time to consider all angles and/or seek out more facts before responding is super helpful. Not only will you spend less energy, you'll have a better chance of controlling your behavior and developing confidence.

Building Self-Confidence and Empowerment

This is done through experience and peer support. Life is pretty unpredictable on a daily basis. Finding ways to recognize your value and knowing you are worthy of being cared for contributes to a sense of confidence; and sometimes meeting a challenge is what strengthens your self-confidence. Taking calculated

Friends who are dealing with similar problems can be a great resource. With the two of you working on a tricky problem, you get twice the possibility to find a helpful and creative solution.

risks, completing hard tasks, learning from mistakes, and forgiving others all contribute to your learning. Befriending buddies who have similar challenges can add to your creativity in finding new paths. The more you know about yourself and your skills, the bigger sense of personal empowerment you will feel. Further, processing events and thinking about the

61

next time keeps you in a growth mind-set. It's forward moving. When you're moving forward, bitterness and resentment can't catch up.

Hope for Yourself and Your Future

You might feel like you're more mature than many teens your age. In some areas, that might be true. In other areas, it won't be. Your brain is a natural thing with its own cycle, and no matter how mature you think you are, you can only grow according to the brain's physical ability at that particular time. For example, a teen's brain is only 80 percent formed by age sixteen, according to the MIT Work-Life Center. And it takes up to ten years after that for its full formation. So, despite being more experienced or knowledgeable in some ways, there are other areas that need to catch up. That's why it's important not to judge others, because you really don't know about them. Stick to your own self and find something you're passionate about. Stay humble. You probably don't know more than others, you just know different things, complemented with different skills. Have faith in yourself and your team, and you will prevail. If you can have hope about change and growth, not much can stop you!

Ways to Deal and Ways to Heal

It's a well-known fact that kids who have a good sense of their abilities tend to handle high stress better and so have a better chance of developing into healthier adults. Developing an ability to bounce back from difficulty—called resilience—is an ongoing process. It happens gradually. Sometimes, it might even feel like you're getting nowhere.

Major Focus for Developing Resilience

You're definitely going to run into lots of stressful situations requiring in-the-moment skills. Fortunately, there has been a lot of research done on kids and resilience. From that research, the American Psychological Association has made a list of ways that adults can help children develop resilience. Here's how that list involves you.

Structure

The most important thing you can work on right now is giving yourself a framework for your daily routine. Making sure your sleeping, eating, and morning routines are relatively consistent will give you a sense of comfort. Be sure to consider all your routines, like waking up your siblings in the morning or packing your book bag at night. Put medications in the same place every day. Arrange the coffee and filter before you go to bed, if possible. In a life where predictability is shifty, defining as much as you can will help beyond measure. Teens have a habit of delaying things to the last minute, though, so beware: procrastination and routine don't mix well!

Consider Short- and Long-Term Goals

If you think about it, nearly everything you do has a goal to it. From choosing your clothes to checking the clock, you have a reason. Another word for reason is goal. You eat to stop hunger pangs. You wash to get clean. You turn in assignments to get grades (short-term goal) and graduate high school (long-term goal). Maybe you work to help the family or to pay for personal stuff. Right now, you probably have a goal to

This family has a reliable morning routine. Routines help to conserve energy and brainpower for use when you really need it.

learn something from reading this book. Or to relieve boredom. Whichever it is, it's a goal. When you can define your goals—the things you want to do, be, or go to—you can begin to map out what you need to get there. You can gather resources and develop your team. You can try some things and evaluate your progress. Track your direction. Tweak as necessary. Arrive!

Social Support and Connectedness

One of the most important things you can do for yourself is develop strong friendships and reach out to your friends for help. Social support is often the biggest factor in successful coping. If you think about it, some things about the experience of having a disabled parent aren't all that easy to describe. But good friends understand things in a way that doesn't always need words. Of course, it's important to choose friends who are responsible and can be trusted with your private information. If you have a friend you trust, who has acted in a consistently dependable way, consider asking that person to help you. A good friend will listen, can help you see different perspectives, and will respectfully tell you when he or she disagrees. And good relationships are a two-way street.

Giving Back

If you have a good friend or two, you know how reassuring it feels to be helped. You can do that for others,

These student volunteers discovered a cool mixture of friends, fun, and service. Volunteering has been shown to fight depression and anxiety, such as by creating feelings of belonging.

too. Several studies have shown that by helping other individuals and the community, the brain produces chemicals that counteract feelings of depression and anxiety. It also creates a sense of belonging. This gives you a place in the world and provides strength and structure for you. It fosters a feeling of acceptance and effectiveness. This is why so many high schools include a requirement for volunteer/community hours. Volunteering helps you get out of your head and see yourself as a part of something much larger. You may find that you want to volunteer with an organization related to your parent's disability, or you may want to do your own thing. Those are both great options, just so long as you're out there volunteering. Giving back helps recipients feel the same kinds of good things. It's a win-win situation.

Stepping Back

Try this: find a picture you're not familiar with. Pick it up without really looking at it and, with your eyes closed, bring the picture all the way up to touch your nose. Open your eyes and try to describe it. You can't, right? Move the picture away from your nose just a little bit. You can see clearer, but not clear enough. Now, move it back a little more. The further away the picture is, the more clearly you can see the details. Life is like that. When you're super involved in something, sometimes you can't see it clearly. Things don't always make sense. Learning to take a step back will change your perspective. It'll give you a chance to relax a little bit. Rest your mind. Do something fun, like learning a new game. Taking some time for yourself is basic to a sense of emotional balance and provides great clarity!

View Change as an Opportunity

Developing a positive attitude is key to moving forward with success. This is because rough stuff happens in life. And so do good things. When you're in a negative mindset, you give more weight to the bad things. The good things can slip out of sight. Positivity, though, breeds hope. It's a way to see ahead and move toward your goals. Use your curiosity to learn about yourself and develop new skills. Life is going to change anyway, and whether you grow from it is up to you. Running away or otherwise avoiding your problems doesn't help in the long term. You can only grow by being present.

Mindfulness for Balance

There is a famous quote that says, "I am a human being, not a human doing." Up until now, you've been focused on what you can do to cope better with your challenges. Being, however, is at least as important as doing. That's where the practice of mindfulness comes in.

Sometimes, your mind is so preoccupied with what you did, what you need to do, and how you're going to do it that you forget about the present moment. Your thoughts can feel miles away, with a to-do list at least as long. Some people experiencing really high stress describe their thoughts and feelings as not being in the room; their body is there, but their brain is turning and twisting about worries in the past or future. It's easy to miss important information, and stress uses valuable energy. Enter mindfulness. This is the practice of focusing your senses to help your mind stay in the present moment. It's a way to recognize where you are and what's happening, without judgment—only knowledge. You can then step back and look at your thoughts and feelings more objectively before acting.

It Simply Is

The common phrase "It is what it is" seems easy to understand, but it's often misused as a statement about giving up. Actually, it's a phrase meant to convey that a situation is simply what it is, without judgment. For example, if it's raining, it's simply raining. That someone says it's a bad day is to attach a judgment to the rain. Once that happens, the mind races ahead to all the things that will be ruined because of the rain. But that doesn't change things; you can't undo or prevent the rain. Judging it or thinking about what the day should have been won't change anything. You still have things to do today. But if you accept the situation, you can calm your body and mind, allowing logic to enter. It takes practice to recognize judgment and choose acceptance. But it can be done. Peace and challenge can exist together

Breathing

Mindfulness helps you train your brain and become more aware of yourself. The first step is to give yourself a chance to recognize your body's felt experience. This begins by paying attention to your breathing.

- Find a comfortable place. The trunk of your body should be relatively straight, with feet crossed or flat on the floor.

Try to take just a few minutes every day to stop, breathe, and listen to the quiet, and then enjoy the immeasurable benefits those few minutes provide.

- With your eyes closed, breathe in and out, deep and slow.
- Now, do it again three more times, listening to your breathing, in and out, deep and slow. Feel your lungs as the breath enters and leaves.
- Just keep breathing—gently in and gently out— for a few minutes. (Some people use a gentle bell or soft song and attend to their breathing until the sound is over.)

After you learn and use this breathing skill, you may notice you feel less negative and perhaps more in control of yourself. You'll then be ready to learn the next skill.

The Five Senses

You may not know it, but each of your senses was developed from a need to survive and adapt. Thus, sight, sound, touch, smell, and taste are all tools humans (and other beings, too) use to detect things like dangerous predators or big mistakes, as well as good-tasting food or bitter poison. Babies put everything in their mouth. They get a lot of information from touching, smelling, tasting, and so forth. So much of what your body tells you goes unnoticed. This second mindfulness skill helps you slow down your mind and detect what's really happening in the room. Take time. Focus on one thing at a time.

- When you're in a comfortable position and breathing gently, notice that your eyes are closed. Is it dark? Can you sense light somewhere?
- Use your ears to listen to your breath gently going in and out. What else can you hear?
- Focus on feeling where the breath goes in your

Attend to your body's language. The body will tell you what it needs before your head does—but only if you listen.

body; attend to whatever you feel with your body. Slowly notice things like the position of your limbs, the texture of your clothing, or the temperature of the room.

- Smell your surroundings—maybe you smell something, maybe nothing. Feel the inhale and exhale. What sorts of things do you smell? A candle? Food? Shampoo? Snow?
- Notice your mouth: is it closed, open a little, dry, comfortable? Can you taste coffee or gum or lunch?
- As you do these things, gently gauge the speed of your breath; it should be nice and even. Is your posture comfortable? Focus slowly. Take your time.

As you strengthen this skill, you want to work on tuning out what's happening around you; just listen to your body. Once you practice and remember to use the breathing and sensing skills, you might notice that you're better able to assess the broader situation. Your choices become clearer, and you'll make better decisions. With mindfulness skills, you can eventually learn to combine emotion and logic, turning it into wisdom.

10 Great Questions to Ask a Mental Health Professional

1. How do I know what to ask my parent and whether it might be insulting?

2. Can my parent pass on his or her disability to me?

3. I get so angry. Am I a bad person?

4. What do I tell my friends?

5. How can I explain my parent's wheelchair?

6. Sometimes, I feel like my parent's parent. Will I always be responsible for him?

7. What is ableism?

8. Mainstreaming is good, right?

9. What are some things I can do to raise awareness about disabilities?

10. What characteristics should I look for in a mental health professional?

CHAPTER SIX

Moving Forward

Never forget that being a teenager can be rough. Each one of you has a particular and unique set of circumstances. And each of you hopefully will make it through adolescence having gained new insight into yourself and others. The best model for growth has to do with keeping an optimistic outlook for yourself while holding a realistic view of your situation, attitude, and resources. If you focus on this goal, you will develop lots of great skills along the way. These skills, as you now know, include empathy, recognizing thinking errors, and developing your voice. You'll run into lots of myths about different kinds of disability. You may feel compelled to correct some, or you may decide it's not worth it in some situations. It's all up to you.

Everyone Should Get Some

One thing that is pretty important to healthy living, which not all teens learn on their way to adulthood, is emotional intelligence (EI). That's what this book has been easing you into. You've learned a little about mindfulness and bringing your emotions and logic together. Emotional intelligence is parallel to that; it develops when you bring your heart and mind together to aid you in recognizing emotions in yourself and in other people. With that information, you can decide how to respond appropriately—taking into account both perspectives. EI doesn't have anything to do with book smarts, and it isn't tangible. It does, however, have some recognizable components you already know.

- **Empathy:** The ability to understand someone's situation from his or her viewpoint; it's useful because it gets you out of your head and expands your knowledge, and it contributes to better decision making.
- **Hope:** A component of motivation toward the future; it helps us see beyond today.
- **Persistence in the face of frustration:** Recognize that the twists and turns of life will throw out roadblocks; it's really annoying, but it's natural. Frustration can make you quit trying for your goals. Learning ways to deal with it will help keep you in the forward-moving, positive

part of learning. The other components look complicated, at first.

- **Delay of gratification/impulse control:** This skill may help prevent a bunch of problems, including wasted resources (like time, money, or energy); broken relationships; and probably even a troublesome reputation. For example, sometimes people do things that make you angry. You may want to scream, curse, be as rude as they were, or hurt them like they hurt you. You imagine it will feel really good to "get" them. You lash out only to find that the person misunderstood, or you did. Or it feels good, but only for a minute. Then you have to do cleanup work. You feel awful and embarrassed. By learning to control your initial impulses, you allow your brain to catch up to the emotion. You don't create a scene. You can manage your reputation a lot better, and people will want to help you, rather than get back at you!

    Giving yourself a little while to think about it takes "payback" out of the realm of impulse. You do this not by talking yourself out of it but by using a distraction skill. If you can think of something else that would also be gratifying, you will be more inclined to breathe deeply and slow your heart rate. Delaying the gratification of impulsive biting words by using distraction helps you see the bigger picture of what's happening.

When you're angry, take time out and allow yourself to feel your feelings in a safe place while waiting for your brain to catch up.

It helps you see how your own thoughts and behaviors affect your path. You'll be able to see a way toward greater success. Lack of impulse control often results in foolishly risky behavior and harmful substance use that can turn into addiction. Instead, use your creativity, grow your imagination, and delay that indulgence in favor of something better and longer lasting.

- **Ability to motivate yourself:** Brain chemicals power motivation. The trick is to figure out how to get those chemicals firing. General things that affect your motivation are sleep, nutrition, focusing on one task at a time, and positive feedback. Of particular importance is the company that you keep. People tend to take on the attitudes and behaviors of people with whom they surround themselves. If you have forward-thinking, positive-minded people on your team, you are more likely to recognize the amount of work you put into something and how to tweak results. Celebrating small steps breeds a positive mind-set. Step-by-step, you ascend the mountain. Choose your climbing partners well.
- **Mood regulation:** As you surely know, your hormones and other brain chemicals are all over the place! Some of it takes time to settle, and some of it is within your control. If you can anticipate things that might happen in a specific situation,

you may be able to think of how to change things for yourself. For example, you can ask a buddy to accompany you to a tough meeting, think up possible responses or solutions beforehand,

After a stressful event, plan something that helps you recuperate, such as going to the perfect place to blow bubbles.

employ empathy, and clarify your goals. If you expect that someone will be rude or disrespectful, you can check in with your body's responses ahead of time and use calming techniques. You can use mindfulness to keep your heart rate low and your attention in the room. You can plan an after event that will feed your spirit.

Developing EI takes commitment. Recognize that when things don't go well, it doesn't mean they never will. (Remember the error of all-or-nothing thinking?) Emotional intelligence is about knowing how things make your body feel so that you can be in charge of your own behavior. But just knowing something isn't enough to cause change; many students can pass a test, but that doesn't mean they can use the material, right? Make people (or yourself) feel something, and you'll have a reason (motivation) for moving forward. Focusing on the previous list of EI components can deliver you to a good place: better personal and professional adjustment. (Fun fact: people with EI tend to have higher salaries per year over people without it. This is because they have a more positive work attitude, spend personal energy better, and have better work output.)

Wow! That's Rad

Researcher, author, and clinician Dr. Marsha Linehan has done groundbreaking work with many difficult

"But" or "And"?

These are two important conjunctions. Each has a dramatically different effect on communication, however. "But" is often referred to as a verbal eraser—anything that comes before it disappears in the meaning of a statement. "And," on the other hand, allows both parts of the sentence to exist together. So, think about how this sentence sounds: "I tried my hardest, *but* it didn't come out well." See how the focus is squarely on the poor result? Now, read the sentence again, and put "and" in place of "but." Notice any difference? "And" allows you to hold both sides of the sentence—you honor yourself by recognizing your hard work, not erasing it. Try other sentences of your own. Do you see how it works?

mental health problems. A most useful principle of her work is that of radical acceptance. Linehan recognized that people were suffering an awful lot because they couldn't accept something that was what it was. She noted that sometimes people don't want to believe something that is true; they spend lots of energy resisting that knowledge. For example, you might want to believe that your parent's symptoms aren't what they are. You might want your parent to throw a ball the way she used to, or to stop blurting out embarrassing things. She can't, but you keep trying to make her. Then you get so mad. It causes you so much frustration or maybe even shame. You use tons of energy trying to force something that can't be; despite what you want, the evidence is undeniable. Refusing to accept a truth can lead you to feel bitter and focus on how unfair the situation is for you. Think of it like hitting a nail from both ends: things might move, but nothing goes anywhere. Nothing changes when nothing changes, right?

Radical acceptance is when you decide to stop resisting and accept what is, not what you want it to be. Think about Molly and the music club she wanted to join. At first, when she was invited to join, she got really mad at her life. She was mean to her siblings because she saw them as big babies who couldn't walk

Sometimes you'll feel annoyed that things aren't what you wish them to be, like for your parent to be symptom free. It's not easy to accept life's tough realities.

home alone from the bus stop. She was angry with her father for being disabled. And she was so tired. Fatigue made her even crabbier. After sharing her feelings with a member of her support team, she came to realize that her situation was what it was: her siblings couldn't miraculously gain age, her father couldn't decide not to have schizophrenia, and her mother didn't have a lot of choice about how to manage her day. What was within Molly's control, however, was shifting her perspective. Once she realized the reality of her situation, she stopped wishing things didn't happen. She came to see that just because she didn't like it didn't mean it wasn't reality. She decided to accept what was and not fight that fight anymore. Then her viewpoint changed. She changed what she wanted. No longer did she demand that her siblings get older instantly or her father change his brain structure. She focused on playing in the band. Once that energy was freed up, she found a different path toward her goal. And it worked!

One detail of great importance is that radical acceptance doesn't mean that you agree with a situation. It isn't about being a sucker or a softy. It's about letting go of wanting to change what can't be changed. You don't have to agree with a situation, you just accept that it is what it is. Once you do that, you can work on changing your thoughts. You turn the energy you were using for overthinking into fuel for forward thinking. Again, this idea takes practice. It's not especially complicated, but it does go against natural tendencies sometimes.

You Need Not Be Alone

Remember, the goal here is to develop a can-do, move-you-forward mentality. The last part of this training is the most important: Choose people wisely. Make a team, and choose people—adults and teens—who will tell it like it is, not what you want to hear. You grow through challenge. Having people you trust to give you their truth, respectfully, is important. You don't have to agree with it, but it'll give you lots to think about.

Of course, if you expect people to tell you the truth, you have to be willing to examine yourself, too. It's important that you review your own thoughts and biases about disability. Don't just talk about something, walk your walk. Your parent may not be able to be the parent you want or expect, but take some time to recognize that he is doing the best he can with the skills and support available. Your parent has worth; it's not less or more than yours, it's just different. It's his own.

Now, the toughest stuff: you are human and so is your parent. Humans do things. They make mistakes, which usually can be understood and/or resolved. Sometimes, though, you might need more serious, scary help. There are situations in which you may find yourself that are not OK. A particular

Sharing similarities and differences respectfully helps you to move through life with a sense of belonging and uniqueness. Friends like these have your back!

subject that people don't talk about much is that of interpersonal abuse. This happens when someone uses physical, mental, emotional, or other forms of manipulation to gain power over you for their benefit. Sadly, far too many children and teens are victims of interpersonal abuse. That abuse can be brought on by all kinds of teens and adults—it doesn't matter if the offender is mainstream or disabled or any other sort of label. Statistically, however, family members far more frequently abuse disabled people than the other way around. Abuse hurts, regardless of intent. Here are two situations in which you might identify abuse:

- **You are being hurt.** For lots of different reasons, disabled or nondisabled parents can sometimes lash out either verbally or physically. You may find yourself being called awful names, blamed for things that didn't happen, inappropriately touched, forced to do things that aren't right, or pushed and hit. Regardless of a person's brain activity, body frustration, or overworked life, these actions are never acceptable. Never. Often teens don't report interpersonal abuse; they may be afraid of what will happen to their family or other relationships, may feel the abuse is justified, may not know how to report it, or may not even know it's abuse.
- **Plenty of research demonstrates the negative**

effects of interpersonal abuse on children and teens. As with disability itself, abuse is complicated to understand, so people often look the other way. They hope it goes away. Remember: you have a right to safety and to have your basic needs met. If this isn't happening for you, it's time to engage a team and explore what can be done. Turn to trusted relatives, school professionals, your therapist, church personnel, and similar people. Abuse just isn't OK.

- **Your parent is being abused.** It is an unfortunate fact that disabled people are often abused as well as exploited for one reason or another. There are always people who value others so little that they can manipulate a disabled person's needs strictly for their own gain. Offenders will see housing, transportation, money, sex, medications, or food as things of value. Disabled people are more often exploited than their mainstream counterparts. Perhaps a disabled parent isn't verbal, becomes easily confused, or makes impulsive decisions. Someone giving her a ride may charge too much, people could pocket medications, or someone could ask to stay just for a few nights but never leave. Even worse, a caretaker could be neglectful. There are all kinds of tricky ways that unscrupulous people can negatively affect the life of a disabled person. If you see something and it doesn't feel right, listen to your intuition. Talk to people. Look up your local disability abuse or domestic abuse hotline. Talk to police. Secrecy won't work here. Some degree of privacy could be maintained, though, if you go about things carefully.

Sometimes, the pressure is overwhelming. It might feel like no matter what you do, you can't affect your life. It can feel like the world is against you. Some teens report feeling so much pressure that they end up doing anything to relieve it, including harmful things like using substances, cutting, sleeping around, or quitting school. Some kids even attempt or complete suicide. The pressure becomes unbearable, and they see no hope in their future. If you've ever felt this way, don't stay silent. Call the National Suicide Prevention Lifeline (1-800-273-8255) or talk to an adult you trust. If you feel like you weren't heard, keep talking and look your adult right in the eyes. Going away and being alone will cause things to keep turning around in your head. Share those things. Let someone help you carry them.

Blooming

Culturally, disability has been seen as something negative. Over the past few decades, however, there has been a movement toward focusing on the positive. For example, a student with attention-deficit/hyperactivity disorder isn't incapable of learning; he just has a different way of learning apart from sitting in a chair all day trying to be "good." A blind person experiences things differently than a seeing person does, with heightened or stronger senses other than sight. The Paralympics are specifically designed for Paralympians. And there are disabled parents who parent differently as well as children who do childhood differently and quite successfully.

Along with this different outlook comes the idea of positive psychology. Indeed, this is a concept of determining what gives a person's life meaning. Researchers like Dr. Martin Seligman wondered how they could help people use their strengths to flourish in their lives. They determined ways to assist people in using the positive aspects of their skill sets to find fulfillment. Positive psychology is a way for people to use the future of possibility as a catalyst toward peaceful living. This is a relatively new concept; rather than seeing different skills as a complement to society, history used to see difference as a disorder to be fixed. Positive psychology compels inclusion. As an important part of that concept, Seligman developed his idea of learned optimism. This is particularly important for kids who have disabled parents. It says

Developing positive, dependable life skills during your teen years will be important in the long run, helping you to develop into a confident adult.

that positivity and optimism aren't predetermined; they can be learned. Thus, negativity can be unlearned.

Here's hoping that there are things for you to learn and ways for you to feel more in control in your life, despite the experience of having a disabled parent, which can sometimes lead to challenges. This resource offers a basic map. Using concepts presented here and reaching out to create a supportive team for yourself should give you a direction for understanding. With understanding can come change and growth. Change happens when you learn to see things, including yourself, from many different angles. Then you have more choices, and with choice comes freedom. Freedom, of course, isn't about having no responsibility. It's about choice. Once you learn and practice all the steps to expand life options for yourself, you can take on any climb with purpose.

ableism A form of discrimination against people with disabilities; can be conscious or unconscious; an ableist sees disabled people as "less than."

adaptive Something that is modified to assist a person in a specific way; can be tangible, like a chair, or a personal skill.

boundary Something that defines a specific limit.

codependent One who is dependent on the needs of another, attending to those needs instead of his or her own.

cultural competency The ability to honor and respect the beliefs, language, interpersonal styles, and behaviors of individuals and families receiving services, as well as of staff who are providing such services.

empathy The ability to be aware of and sensitive to the thoughts and feeling of another.

empowerment The process of enabling one's personal influence over self.

felt experience The emotional, personal, and cognitive evaluation of a situation, apart from reality, as interpreted by the person experiencing it.

interpersonal abuse When individuals use their greater personal power over another as a means of hurting or controlling that person; particularly in the mental, emotional, physical, sexual, and financial areas.

learned optimism The idea that joy can be consciously learned.

mainstream The prevailing direction; majority.

mindfulness In-the-moment, nonjudgmental awareness of person, place, and thing.

Paralympian Someone who competes in the Paralympics, an Olympic-style sporting event specifically for disabled athletes.

parity Equality among the parts.

positive psychology A theory that views mental functioning in light of an individual's differences in terms of strengths, rather than as illness.

psychophobia The fear of psychological differences, which leads to a form of discrimination and prejudice.

resilience The ability to bounce back from failure or disappointment through adaptation as a means of dealing effectively with changing circumstances.

service provider A person who provides a specific service in a professional capacity.

social support The idea or reality that a person is cared for and can rely on certain others.

status quo The status of keeping things as they currently are; no change.

stigma A negative connotation attached to one who has or is believed to have some attribute that is depreciative in nature; the person is seen as inferior.

thinking errors Irrational patterns of thinking that tend to distort reality.

trust A feeling formed when, over time, another person is seen to be honest and reliable.

WD-40 A multipurpose lubricant sold worldwide.

For More Information

Americans with Disabilities Act (ADA)

US Department of Justice

950 Pennsylvania Ave. NW

Civil Rights Division

Disability Rights Section—NYA

Washington, DC 20530

(202) 514-0301

TTY/SCDII/TDD: (800) 514-0383

Website: https://www.ada.gov

Facebook: @civilrights

This website provides an introduction to the ADA. It also lists hotline numbers that allow people to talk to someone in person.

Canadian Disability Policy Alliance

Abramsky Hall

21 Arch Street, 3rd Floor

Queen's University

Kingston, ON K7L 3N6

Canada

(613) 533-6000

Email: contact@disablitypolicyalliance.ca

Website: http://www.disabilitypolicyalliance.ca

Facebook: @canadiandisabilityalliance

Twitter: @CDAdisability22

Instagram: @canadian.disability.alliance

This organization provides newsletters, presentations, and publications about disability issues important to Canadian residents. The website offers a link to the Canadian Disability Act as well as to several research articles.

Canadian Mental Health Association

500-250 Dundas Street W.

Toronto, ON M5T 2Z5

Canada

(800) 875-6213

Email: info@ontario.cmha.ca

Website: https://www.ontario.cmha.ca

Facebook: @cmha.ontario

Twitter: @CDAdisability22

Instagram: @cmhaceh

This volunteer association provides advocacy, education, research, and service for people experiencing mental health challenges. Its website also offers links to local chapters within the Canadian provinces.

National Alliance on Mental Illness

3803 North Fairfax Drive, Suite 100

Arlington, VA 22203

(703) 524-7600

Email: contact@disablitypolicyalliance.ca

Website: https://www.nami.org

Facebook: @nami

Twitter and Instagram: @namicommunicate

This organization provides service to millions of Americans affected by mental illness. It has multiple state- and city-level chapters offering support and education, with a number of programs geared both for people living with mental illness and for their family, friends, and caregivers. The website also offers specific information on a number of different mental illnesses.

National Child Abuse Hotline

4350 East Camelback Road, Building F250

Phoenix, AZ 85018

(480) 422-8212

Hotline: (800) 422-4453

Email: Accessible online via forms at https://www .childhelp.org/contact

Website: http://www.childhelp.org

Facebook, Twitter, and Instagram: @childhelp

This US organization works on prevention, intervention, treatment, and community outreach regarding child abuse and neglect, as well as at-risk children.

National Disability Rights Network

820 First Street NE, Suite 740

Washington, DC 20002

(202) 408-9514

TTY: (202) 408-9521

Email: info@ndrn.org

Website: http://www.ndrn.org

Facebook and Twitter: @NDRNadvocates

The National Disability Rights Network offers educational resources as well as training and advocacy for those with disabilities.

National Suicide Prevention Lifeline

Substance Abuse and Mental Health Services Administration

5600 Fishers Lane

Rockville, MD 20257

(877) 726-4727

TTY: (800) 487-4889

Hotline: (800) 273-8255

Website: https://suicidepreventionlifeline.org

Facebook and Twitter: @800273TALK

This group offers support and resources for those contemplating suicide. It also works to increase public awareness regarding suicide prevention.

Students Against Destructive Decisions (SADD)

1440 G Street

Washington, DC 20005

(508) 481-3568

TTY: (800) 487-4889

Hotline: (800) 273-8255

Email: Accessible online via forms at http://www .sadd.org/contact-sadd

Website: http://www.sadd.org

Facebook and Twitter: @SADDnation

The SADD website offers peer-to-peer education, prevention, and activism geared toward preventing destructive decisions, particularly underage drinking, drug use, risky and impaired driving, teen violence, and teen suicide.

Substance Abuse and Mental Health Services Administration (SAMHSA)

5600 Fishers Lane

Rockville, MD 20257

(877) 726-4727

TTY: (800) 487-4889

Website: https://www.samhsa.gov

Facebook: @samhsa

Twitter: @samhsagov

The SAMHSA website offers information regarding a myriad of substance abuse and mental health disorders and life areas touched by them. It also has a great section of free or low-cost publications.

For Further Reading

Alberti, Robert, and Michael Emmons. *Your Perfect Right: Assertiveness and Equality in Your Life and Relationships.* Oakland, CA: New Harbinger Publications, 2017.

Alvord, Mary Karapetian, and Ann McGrath. *Conquer Negative Thinking for Teens: A Workbook to Break the Nine Thought Habits That Are Holding You Back.* Oakland, CA: Instant Help Books, 2017.

Baruch-Feldman, Caren, and Thomas Hoerr. *The Grit Guide for Teens: A Workbook to Help You Build Perseverance, Self-Control, and a Growth Mindset.* Oakland, CA: Instant Help Books, 2017.

Covey, Steven. *The 6 Most Important Decisions You'll Ever Make: A Guide for Teens.* New York, NY: Fireside Publishing, 2006.

Freedman, Jeri. *Your Beautiful Brain: Keeping Your Brain Healthy.* New York, NY: Rosen Publishing, 2013.

Hoffman, Bobby. *Hack Your Motivation: Over 50 Science-Based Strategies to Improve Performance.* Oviedo, FL: Attribution Press. 2017.

Huddle, Lorena, and Jay Schlifer. *Teen Suicide.* New York, NY: Rosen Publishing, 2012.

Kabat-Zinn, Jon. *Mindfulness for Beginners:*

Reclaiming the Present Moment and Your Life. Boulder, CO: Sounds True, 2016.

Klein, Stanley, and John Kemp. *Reflections from a Different Journey: What Adults with Disabilities Wish All Parents Knew.* New York, NY: McGraw-Hill, 2011.

Schab, Lisa. *The Anxiety Workbook for Teens: Activities to Help You Deal with Anxiety and Worry.* Oakland, CA: Instant Help Books, 2008.

Bibliography

Alvord, Mary Karapetian, and Anne McGrath. *Conquer Negative Thinking for Teens: A Workbook to Break the Nine Tough Habits That Are Holding You Back.* Oakland, CA: Instant Help Books, 2017.

American Psychological Association, Psychology Help Center. "Resilience Guide for Parents & Teachers." 2017. http://www.apa.org/helpcenter /resilience.aspx.

Americans with Disabilities Act of 1990. Public Law 101-336. 108th Congress, 2nd session (July 26, 1990).

Beck, Arron. "Cognitive Therapy: Nature and Relation to Behavior Therapy." *Behavior Therapy* 1, no. 2 (1970): 184–200.

Center on the Developing Child, Harvard University, "Key Concepts in Resilience." 2017. https://developingchild.harvard.edu/science /key-concepts/resilience.

Ginsburg, Kenneth, and Martha Jablow. *Building Resilience in Children and Teens: Giving Kids Roots and Wings.* 3rd. ed. Grove Village, IL: American Academy of Pediatrics, 2015.

Kauffman, Scott Barry, with Caren Baruch-Feldman. "99: Growing Grit in Teens." *The Psychology Podcast*, August 9, 2017. https://podcast.party /podcasts/the-psychology-podcast-with-dr -scott-barry-kaufman/99-growing-grit-in -teens.

Linehan, Marsha. "Marsha Linehan, Ph.D., ABPP— Balancing Acceptance and Change: DBT and the Future of Skills Training." Family Action Network, November 17, 2015. https://www .youtube.com/watch?v=JMUk0TBWASc.

MIT Work-Life Center. "Welcome." Accessed November 20, 2017. http://hrweb.mit.edu /worklife.

National Institute of Mental Health. *The Teen Brain: 6 Things to Know.* NIH Publication No. OM 16-4307. https://www.nimh.nih.gov/health /publications/the-teen-brain-6-things-to -know/index.shtml.

Ozbay, F., D.C. Johnson, E. Dimoulas, C.A. Morgan, D. Charney, and S. Southwick. "Social Support and Resilience to Stress: From Neurobiology to Clinical Practice." *Psychiatry (Edgmont)* 4, no. 5 (2007): 35–40.

Seligman, Martin. *The Optimistic Child: A Proven Program to Safeguard Children from Depression and Build Lifelong Resilience.* New York, NY: Houghton Mifflin, 1996.

United States Census Bureau. "Nearly 1 in 5 People Have a Disability in the U.S., Census Bureau Reports." July 25, 2012. https://www.census.gov /newsroom/releases/archives/miscellaneous /cb12-134.html.

Index

About the Author

Dr. Mary P. Donahue earned her doctoral degree in counseling psychology from the University at Albany, State University of New York. She maintains a clinical practice specializing in grief and trauma with both adolescents and adults. Dr. Donahue and her family work and play worldwide while living happily in southern Maine.

About the Expert

H. Ace Ratcliff is a disability rights activist, writer, photographer, and artist living in incredible Oakland, California, with their fiancé and their pack of wild beasts. They love museums, photography adventures, dogs, and all combinations thereof. They tweet @stayweirdbekind. Learn more at http://www.stayweirdbekind.com.

Photo Credits

Cover Miriam Doerr Frommherz/Shutterstock.com; p. 5 realpeople/Shutterstock.com; p. 9 Jovanmandic/iStock/Thinkstock; p. 11 Tom Wang/Shutterstock.com; p. 13 Highwaystarz-Photography/iStock/Thinkstock; p. 16 © iStockphoto.com/asiseeit; p. 18 Jetta Productions/Photodisc/Thinkstock; p. 25 XiXinXing/iStock/Thinkstock; pp. 26–27 © iStockphoto.com/cezars; p. 31 IvanMiladinovic/iStock/Thinkstock; pp. 32–33 © iStockphoto.com/golero; p. 35 SolStock/E+/Getty Images; p. 39 serts/E+/Getty Images; p. 41 © iStockphoto.com/pixelheadphoto; pp. 46–47 Mixmike/E+/Getty Images; p. 49 © iStockphoto.com/digitalskillet; p. 53 © iStockphoto.com/eugenesergeev; p. 56 © iStockphoto.com/MangoStar_Studio; p. 59 © iStockphoto.com/Guasor; p. 61 fstop123/E+/Getty Images; p. 65 © iStockphoto.com/TAGSTOCK1; p. 67 Wavebreakmedia Ltd/Thinkstock; p. 71 © iStockphoto.com/FatCamera; p. 73 © iStockphoto.com/paulaphoto; p. 79 Juanmonino/E+/Getty Images; p. 81 Jasmina007/E+/Getty Images; pp. 84–85 © iStockphoto.com/Juanmonino; p. 88 DGLimages/iStock/Thinkstock; p. 93 splendens/iStock/Thinkstock.

Design and Layout: Nicole Russo-Duca; Editor and Photo Researcher: Heather Moore Niver